How to Keep Your Kids DRUG FREE

Robert Morey

HARVEST HOUSE PUBLISHERS
Eugene, Oregon 97402

Except where otherwise indicated, all Scripture quotations in this book are taken from the New American Standard Bible, ©1960, 1962, 1963, 1968, 1971, 1972, 1973, 1975, 1977 by The Lockman Foundation. Used by permission.

Verses marked KJV are taken from the King James Version of the Bible.

HOW TO KEEP YOUR KIDS DRUG-FREE

Copyright © 1993 by Dr. Robert A. Morey
Published by Harvest House Publishers
Eugene, Oregon 97402

Library of Congress Cataloging-in-Publication Data

Morey, Robert A., 1946-
  How to keep your kids drug free / Robert Morey.
    p. cm.
  Originally published: Southbridge, MA: Crowne Publications. ©1989.
  Includes bibliographical references and index.
  ISBN 1-56507-088-7
  1. Children—United States—Drug use. 2. Drug abuse —
United States—Prevention. 3. Drug abuse—Religious
aspects—Christianity. 4. Child rearing—Religious
aspects—Christianity. I. Title.
  HV5824,C45M67 1993
  649',4—dc20   92-44139
                                                      CIP

Printed in the United States of America.

CONTENTS

BEFORE YOU
BEGIN...

The modern drug abuse movement is evangelistic about its "gospel."

And the evangelists who are spreading that gospel might surprise you. They aren't limited to the likes of Timothy Leary and Alan Watts, who became known in the sixties because of their enthusiastic and zealous propagation of the chemical gospel.

Today's movement is riding on the tidal wave of a renewed preoccupation with Eastern religions, philosophies, and occultic practices.

Since drug use is considered a vital part of the Eastern religious experience, we can expect an increase in drug activity to take place as more and more people seek meaning in life from Eastern mysticism.

So once again, as in the sixties, Western society is confronted with the questions, What is wrong in using drugs? Isn't it okay to enjoy the freedom and experience offered by drugs as long as you are not hurting anyone else?

Christian parents must equip themselves to answer those questions, not only to protect their children, but also because they are under the divine mandate from their Lord to always be ready "to make a defense to every one who asks you to give an account for the hope that is in you" (1 Peter 3:15).

It is in response to the Lord's command that this book is written. It will attempt to bring into sharper focus the biblical data relevant to the subject of drugs. It is hoped this will enable pastors, parents, teachers, and young people to answer the knotty questions drug users ask.

This book will be limited to the biblical, theological, and ethical issues involved in the use of drugs for non-medical purposes. This limitation is justifiable because hundreds of reports have already been done on the clinical and chemical aspect of drug abuse. However, when searching for works which discuss what the Bible says about drugs, one finds relatively few sources.

The procedure of this study is to interpret all human experiences in the light of the infallible Scriptures. That's because the only authority in all matters of life, faith, and practice is the Bible, which is the Word of God. All other considerations are subordinate to the Scriptures.

The topics that make up this book have arisen out of several years' experience in working with drug users in the Greenwich Village section of New York City. During that time the biblical answers to drug abuse presented in this book had their "trial by fire" in many serious discussions with drug users. Thankfully, God has used this study in the rehabilitation of many who were addicted to drugs.

It is with the prayer and support of the people of God that this book is published. May the kingdom of Christ advance by the truth of the gospel.

Chapter 1

WHY DO PEOPLE
TAKE DRUGS?

How is the "Just Say No" generation faring?

Undoubtedly, the fight for a drug-free America gained a lot of mileage from that short, catchy slogan.

Yet the country is still far from drug-free. Though the psychedelic sixties and partying seventies are but memories, drugs have endured into the nineties. They are now considered a vital part of certain Eastern religious or occultic practices which have recently taken Western society by storm.

It is clear that drugs are able to transcend the fads in which they play a part. Though the rock music scene of the sixties and the Eastern mysticism of today are worlds apart, something has compelled the participants of both worlds to abuse drugs.

Why do people take drugs? The answer is not as obvious as some suppose. That question should be broken into two parts: 1. Why do people *initially* try drugs? and 2. Why do people *continue* to use drugs?

Why do people initially try drugs? Drug users usually respond by saying that they first tried drugs because of social pressure, boredom, or curiosity, desire of a new experience, better sex, greater wisdom or intelligence, or an escape from pain, worry, responsibility, tension, and so on.

Upon examination, it is clear that some of the motivations underlying a person's initial use of drugs arise out of varied natural, normal, or sociologically conditioned needs or desires.

In this sense, drug abuse can be viewed as one way in which man attempts to satisfy his needs or desires. This is why drug abuse is so appealing and popular. It draws on certain natural desires of man and is favored by a certain sociological and religious climate which is conducive to drug abuse.

While it is true that drug abuse may be motivated by certain needs of man, this does not mean that it is therefore beneficial. We must seriously consider that man has two radically different sets of desires from totally opposite origins.

Man was created by God. But he was not created as a self-contained, autonomous robot without any needs or desires. Man had real created needs and desires. For example, after God created Adam He said, "It is not good for the man to be alone; I will make him a helper suitable for him" (Genesis 2:18). Thus the desire and need for human companionship, communication, and love are *created* desires. These desires can be traced back to the creation of man by God.

After a period of testing, man sinned and as a result developed certain needs and desires which cry out for satisfaction. These needs and desires are sinful in their origin and goal. For example, the desire to kill one's self or other people can be traced back to the Fall of man into sin. This desire is not a part of man's original creation but it is a *sinful* desire.

When seeking to deal with the reasons underlying drug abuse, the created desires should be isolated from the sinful desires. Then it should be pointed out that God has provided wonderful ways in which all the created desires of man can be satisfied within the prescribed limits set by His revealed will. This means that one does not need to turn to drugs to satisfy his natural needs.

By distinguishing between created and sinful needs, we can refute and reject those who legitimize drug abuse on the grounds that it fulfills some natural need or desire of man. Some have compared man's need for the drug experience with his need for food or sleep.[1] But the desire for food or sleep comes from man's creation, while the desire for the drug experience comes from the Fall of man into sin and guilt.

Why do people continue to use drugs? When asked this question, most drug users do not give any of the initial reasons for trying drugs. They have now found a new and deeper motivation for drug abuse. Drugs are viewed as a means by which one can experience a certain mental state. Certain drugs can produce a state of seemingly expanded consciousness and allow one to experience a totally different world of perception. To enter into an abnormal mental state becomes the sole motivation of the typical drug user. Regardless if he wants to go up or down or way out, he wants a different mental state than the one experienced when he is not on drugs.

What is the drug experience? The following description points out some of the usual or general side effects in all drug experiences. Some people have experienced all the side effects at one time; others have experienced only some of them over a period of time.

In every drug experience a person loses something. During that time one alters the straight or normal way of thinking and as a result may lose:

1. the ability to understand things rationally.
2. contact with the normal world of sense perception.
3. any accurate perception of the size, shape, or color of objects.
4. the ability to perceive differences between objects.

5. the sense of self and its identity.
6. the awareness of time.
7. consciousness of the past and its importance.
8. consciousness of the future and its goals.
9. the ability to give sustained attention.
10. the ability to communicate intelligently.

In every drug experience a person is subject
to certain delusions. These include:

1. the sensation of having great insight, in-
   tuition, and knowledge.
2. a monistic or pantheistic perception of
   the universe.
3. an experience of godhood by sensing
   that one is infinite, omniscient, omnipo-
   tent, indestructible, and eternal.
4. the sense of being possessed, overpow-
   ered, or carried along by some force
   greater than oneself.
5. a heightened perception of sounds, sights,
   and colors.
6. a heightened sensual experience of sex,
   touch, and taste.
7. a confusion of the senses in which one
   may see music and hear colors.
8. the ability to live in the present without
   any care of concern for the past or future.
9. the ability to be released from all responsibility and restraint and to do whatever
   one feels like doing.
10. mystical or religious experiences with
    God or spiritual beings.

These are most of the delusions which accompany a drug experience.[2]

What can be said about the altered mental state? Is it good or bad? Is it beneficial for man or destructive? The answers to these questions will decide the issue of drug abuse.

Some people mistakenly think that the best way to fight drug abuse is to demonstrate scientifically the harmful effects of drugs. The government-sponsored, drug-abuse educational programs have used this method and failed miserably.[3] These people do not realize that by basing all their objections to drug abuse on a scientific demonstration of the harmful effects of drugs on the body, they are opening the door for the legalization of drug abuse. They will have no basis or right to reject the legalization of a drug which may be discovered or invented in the future which does not cause any physical harm.

While the harmful effects of drugs do play an important role in the fight against drug abuse, the primary attack should be made against the major motivation and goal of drug abuse: the state of an altered or heightened consciousness. This is where the battle must be carried out and won.

One of the most eloquent defenders of the drug abuse movement, Andrew Weil, has attempted to legitimize drug abuse on the grounds that it releases a person from the straight world and brings one into a state of expanded consciousness. He feels that this state is better than "straight thinking."[4] Timothy Leary, commenting on Weil's work, put forth his "Hedonic Psychology," in which drugs play a major role in introducing man to another world of perception.[5] For such people, drugs are just one of many means to arrive at a desired state. For Leary, Watts, and Weil, the end justifies the means. They not only condone drug abuse but recommend it.

Once it is realized that the central issue in drug abuse is the drug experience itself, we can then say anything which produces this altered mental state must be condemned. This condemnation would stand even if a drug is discovered which is physically harmless and non-addictive.

It must also be pointed out that there are ways to produce an altered mental state in man other than by the use of drugs. The Eastern mystics use yoga, meditation, chanting, singing, and dancing to get their "high." The mystical experience for which they strive is exactly the same as a drug-induced experience and stands under the same condemnation.

Only biblical Christianity can supply the proper arguments against the issue of the drug experience. Since this requires an accurate knowledge of biblical Christianity, let's examine the foundational truths of Christianity and apply them to the subject of drug abuse and the drug experience.

Chapter 2

DRUGS AND THE BIBLICAL CONCEPT OF CREATION

The Bible reveals three basic concepts by which all of life must be interpreted. These are the Creation, the Fall, and Redemption. They make up the basis of the Christian worldview. To interpret and to understand anything in the light of the Bible is to see it in the light of the Creation, the Fall, and Redemption.

Perhaps upon reading the title of this chapter you are tempted to ask, "Why are you beginning with a basic concept such as the doctrine of Creation? What does the creation of the heavens and the earth have to do with the subject of drugs?"

There are four principal reasons to discuss drugs in the light of the biblical doctrine of Creation. First, we are now living in what has been described as a "post-Christian" age. Religious liberalism and scientism have largely removed the truth of Creation from the thinking of Western man.

Second, because of the popular influx of Eastern religions and the influence of modern philosophies and theologies, a concept of pantheism (the doctrine that the universe is God) has replaced the Christian concept of Creation in the minds of many people. This is particularly true of today's young people. Many of them have never heard of Creation and have been taught that everything and everyone is a part of God.

Third, the concept of pantheism functions for many as the basis for taking drugs, and has an important role in the interpretation of the drug experience. Popular leaders, such as Watts or Leary, have embraced pantheism and have strongly influenced the whole drug movement toward Eastern concepts of pantheism. The popular ecological movement is using pantheism in its propaganda.[1]

Fourth, unless you understand the biblical doctrine of Creation, you can never understand the rest of Scripture, for without the Creation doctrine as a basis, you cannot understand crucial biblical teaching on the Fall of man into sin or the Redemption of man by Christ. Therefore, it is imperative to begin with the biblical doctrine of Creation in opposition to the concept of pantheism.[2]

What is the concept of Creation as given to us in the Bible? According to the Scriptures, the true God is uncreated and eternal. "Before the mountains were brought forth, or ever thou hadst formed the earth and the world, even from everlasting to everlasting, thou art God" (Psalm 90:2 KJV). However, time, matter, energy, space, and all other things had a beginning and are not eternal. "In the beginning God created the heavens and the earth" (Genesis 1:1).

By an act of His sovereign free will, God created everything without using pre-existent material. Nor did He form the universe from His own being, nature, or essence. The Creator and His creation are totally and qualitatively distinct from one another because God is infinite and the creation is finite. They do not in any way participate in the same scale of being. The universe is not God or a part of God. It is the creation of God (John 1:1-4; Colossians 1:16,17; Hebrews 11:3; Revelation 4:11). To call or worship any part of created reality as God is to be an idolator (Romans 1:18-32).

Because God created all things, everything is intrinsically good. "And God saw all that He had made, and behold, it was very good" (Genesis 1:31). Thus matter and all things which are created cannot be understood as being evil in and of themselves. Therefore, Christians do not reject any creature, plant, drink, or drug on the grounds that it is intrinsically evil. We believe that everything God has created is good (Matthew 15:1-11; Acts10:9-15; I Corinthians 10:26-31; I Timothy 4:1-5).

The universe was not only created good but was also created with a divine purpose. God has a definite purpose for everything He created (Psalm 19; Proverbs 16:4; Revelation 4:11). There is no contingency or meaninglessness beneath or behind the universe. Nothing happens by chance or luck. God placed man on the earth to use all of created reality in its divinely ordained functions (Genesis 1, 2; Ecclesiastes 3:1-15; Revelation 4:11). Man's duty is to discover the right use of each created thing and to use it only for the purpose for which God has created it. We must therefore look upon every plant, drink, and drug as having some purpose and function in created reality.

Once the biblical doctrine of Creation is understood and believed, any pantheistic basis for a drug experience or pantheistic interpretation of that experience will be rejected. While using drugs, a person may be deceived by his hallucinations to think that he has become one with God or a part of God. Some claim to see the universe as a divine organism which lives and breathes. Another popular deception during a drug experience is that a person can become one with the objects around him. Some testify that they became one with a flower or a light bulb. One individual even claimed that he became a musical note and was caught up into a Bach cantata!

We cannot deny that people can have such mental deceptions during a drug experience. But Scripture forbids the pantheistic interpretation of such experiences. The Bible gives us a theistic interpretation of reality, which maintains the radical distinction between the Creator and His creation. Man cannot become God through chemicals or any other means. Nor can he merge into one being with created objects. Man cannot become a flower. God created man to be a man, and he will always be a man—though at times a deceived man.[3]

Since Christians hold to the doctrine of Creation, they do not have the negative attitude toward matter that Eastern religions maintain. The Eastern pantheist wants to get away from the body and life in this world. He wants to escape to an inner world of nonmaterial reality because he views the world as evil. In contrast, only in the doctrine of Creation do we find a positive attitude toward material reality.

Similarly, because pantheism encourages escape to some "Nirvana," it cannot use drugs for the right purpose. Only the doctrine of Creation can serve as a basis for the positive, useful, and correct use of the drugs which God created.

Chapter 3

DRUGS AND THE BIBLICAL CONCEPT OF THE FALL

Now that we have viewed the biblical concept of Creation, we come to the second concept: the radical fall of man into sin and guilt.

God created man righteous, pure, and holy (Genesis 1, 2). Man, however, did not remain in this condition. He rebelled against his Creator and became wicked and corrupt before God. The original sin of Adam and Eve in the Garden of Eden was not, as some men suppose, the act of sex. The Bible clearly teaches that sex was created by God. Before Adam and Eve fell into sin, God commanded them to procreate: "And God blessed them; and God said to them, 'Be fruitful and multiply, and fill the earth, and subdue it; and rule over the fish of the sea and over the birds of the sky, and over every living thing that moves on the earth'" (Genesis 1:28).

The original sin was an act of rebellion against God's clear command to not eat the fruit of the tree of the knowledge of good and evil. God allowed Adam to eat of any tree in the garden except for this one tree (Genesis 2:16, 17).

Adam and Eve listened to the word of Satan instead of obeying the Word of God. Because they ate the forbidden fruit, they were driven from the garden as punishment (Genesis 3). Thus the original sin was the rebellion of man in misusing a part of the creation to satisfy the evil desires of his heart.

The sin of Adam had two effects. First, it made him legally guilty before God because he had broken God's law. Thus man became the object of God's just and holy anger. Second, Adam's sin infected his own being and made him evil. Man became corrupt in every facet of his nature. The Bible teaches that all men are born with an evil nature (Psalm 51:5; Romans 1:5; Ephesians 2:1-3) and that "all have sinned and fall short of the glory of God" (Romans 3:23). No aspect of man escapes the radical effects of the Fall. In his emotional, intellectual, and volitional activities, man is a sinner before the true God.[1]

Because man is now totally depraved in his thoughts, feelings, and desires, he lives out this depravity in every area of experience. In relation to God, sin is disobedience to His holy law and Word (1 John 3:4). Sin is any form of idolatry (Exodus 20:3-7). In relation to the world around man, sin is the abuse and misuse of the creation in opposition to the directive to God's law (Exodus 20:8-17). Thus the source of man's abuse or misuse of any created object is the depravity of his own nature. Man perverts the use of certain plants, drinks, and drugs that God created for man's good, and turns them into sinful tools that he uses to hurt himself and his neighbor.

This means that a person does not become a drug abuser primarily because of adverse sociological or psychological factors. These factors are important, but they are not the ultimate cause of drug abuse. From the Christian perspective, drug abuse does not arise from man's ignorance or residence but from his sinfulness.

Sin is the ultimate cause of all of man's problems. The failure to see this has resulted in misguided attempts to help drug users. Unless we lay the axe to the root, we cannot expect a radical cure. Therefore, if a person is serious about getting off drugs, he must see drug abuse as something sinful. The task before him is that of truly repenting from sin. This repentance involves turning away from sin with all of his being while calling upon God for deliverance through Jesus Christ.

The validity and truthfulness of this view was illustrated at a well-known Christian drug-abuse center in Brooklyn, New York. Several men from the FBI came in and started asking questions. In conversation, one of them said that the government could not officially send anyone to a religious organization even for drug rehabilitation. However, so many drug users had been cured at this Christian establishment that they had come to see the secret of the success. After the Gospel was explained to them, they replied that although the government could not allow religion as a part of rehabilitation, they were going to send people to the center unofficially. Certain individuals with whom the government had worked and failed came to the center. There they became converted and seemed permanently cured of drug abuse. Obviously, the power of the Gospel had been displayed to the government officials.

Chapter 4

DRUGS AND THE BIBLICAL CONCEPT OF REDEMPTION

The third biblical concept by which we understand the world is Redemption. God's redemption through Jesus Christ is the major theme of the entire Bible. It can be said that the Bible is the Book of Redemption. There are four basic characteristics of the biblical concept of Redemption in the teaching of the Bible.[1]

First of all, redemption was planned and accomplished by God. He was not taken by surprise when man fell into sin. God already had a plan of salvation for man before He created the universe: "He chose us in Him before the foundation of the world, that we should be holy and blameless before Him" (Ephesians 1:4).

Second, redemption is Trinitarian. Each member of the Godhead is involved in redemption. God the Father planned the salvation of sinners by electing or choosing them unto salvation (2 Thessalonians 2:13). He sent His Son to redeem the ones He had chosen (John 17:2). God the Son came to die on the cross to pay the full penalty for the sins of the people of God (Hebrews 2:17). He died in their place to secure eternal redemption for them (1 John 4:10). Then the Father and the Son sent the Holy Spirit to apply Christ's redemption to those for whom He died. Thus, Christians were chosen by the Father, purchased by the Son, and sealed by the Spirit. Salvation is from the Triune God.

Third, redemption concerns individual persons. It is personal as opposed to all the modern forms of impersonalism. God originally created mankind as individual people. As individual persons mankind fell into sin. As individual persons sinners are saved. God the Father elected individual persons (John 6:37,65), and God the Spirit renews and indwells individual persons (Ephesians 1:13). This is not to deny the biblical concept of the body of Christ; remember that even this body is made up of individual units (1 Peter 2:5). Thus God deals with each sinner individually and personally.

Fourth, God's plan of redemption is cosmic in scope. In addition to there being in heaven a multitude of the redeemed which no man can number, the earth itself is to be delivered from the effects of the radical fall into sin. Romans 8:19-23 (KJV) tells us about that:

> For the earnest expectation of the creature waiteth for the manifestation of the sons of God. For the creature

was made subject to vanity, not will-
ingly, but by reason of him who hath
subjected the same in hope, Because
the creature itself also shall be delivered from the bondage of corruption
into the glorious liberty of the children of God. For we know that the
whole creation groaneth and travail-
eth in pain together until now. And
not only they, but ourselves also,
who have the firstfruits of the Spirit,
even we ourselves groan within ourselves, waiting for the adoption, to
wit, the redemption of our body.

Second Peter 3:7-17 (KJV) says there will
one day be a new heaven and earth where there
is no pollution or contamination from sin:

But the heavens and the earth, which
are now, by the same word are kept
in store, reserved unto fire against
the day of judgment and perdition of
ungodly men. But, beloved, be not
ignorant of this one thing, that one
day is with the Lord as a thousand
years, and a thousand years as one
day. The Lord is not slack concerning his promise, as some men count
slackness; but is longsuffering to us-
ward, not willing that any should
perish, but that all should come to

repentance. But the day of the Lord
will come as a thief in the night; in
the which the heavens shall pass away
with a great noise, and the elements
shall melt with fervent heat, the earth
also and the works that are therein
shall be burned up. Seeing then that
all these things shall be dissolved,
what manner of persons ought ye to
be in all holy conversation and god-
liness, looking for and hasting unto
the coming of the day of God, wherein the heavens being on fire shall be
dissolved, and the elements shall melt
with fervent heat? Nevertheless we,
according to his promise, look for new
heavens and a new earth, wherein
dwelleth righteousness.

With this basic understanding of biblical
redemption, it is obvious that biblical Christianity stands opposed to any Eastern, pantheistic concept of the ultimate destruction of the
individual person by absorption into the One.[2]
The Eastern belief in annihilation of the individual self is a popular explanation of certain
drug-induced experiences. Some have even
thought of their annihilation in terms of the
"salvation" of man. This impersonal annihilistic
doctrine is the cause of many suicide attempts.

One young man convinced himself that his
"salvation" awaited the destruction of his indi-

vidual self. Upon death he would be absorbed into the One. He attempted suicide three times, but then the sovereign grace of God rescued him. He now knows that true salvation consists in the restoration of man in the image of God. As a created, individual human being, he looks forward to eternally worshipping his Creator and Redeemer.

Chapter 5

THE CHRISTIAN WORLDVIEW OF DRUG ABUSE

Having outlined the biblical concepts of the Creation, the Fall, and Redemption as normative for interpreting the drug experience, we can begin to articulate our thesis.

On the basis of what has been said, it should be clear that we are dealing with antithesis between right and wrong. Therefore it is imperative to come to grips with the basis of Christian ethics, which is summarized as follows: Something is wrong when God says it is wrong in His Word, the Holy Scriptures.[1] This means that we must examine the Scriptures in order to know the thoughts of God concerning drug experience.

Perhaps some who place their own limited, subjective experience above the authority of the inspired Word of God will disagree with much of what is about to be said. May you be open-minded concerning the biblical interpretation and evaluation of your experience.

One problem we are faced with is clarifying the distinction between the medical use of drugs and the abusive use of drugs. At this point, it is wise to explain what this distinction is and why it is made.

The New Testament records over one hundred cases of healing. Most of these healings were miracles performed by Christ and His apostles by the power of the Holy Spirit (John 5:2-9; 1 Corinthians 12:9,28). However, Christ portrayed himself as a physician and, in doing so, He described some of the functions of a physician (Mark 2:17). Taking the teaching of Christ in the Gospels, we can construct a biblical view of the primary task of a physician to indicate some of the functions of his medicines.

"They that be whole need not a physician, but they that are sick" (Matthew 9:12 KJV). The function of drugs for medical purposes is to bring a person from the abnormal state of sickness or unwholeness into a state of normal health. God has graciously given to man the means to cure diseases. However, drug abuse functions to take a person from the normal state of life into an abnormal state. On this we can all agree, without stating whether this drug-induced abnormal state is good or bad.

The medical use of drugs strives to bring a non-functioning person back to being a functioning person in society. The aim is to make a man well and to return him to his family and his work.

On the other hand, this is manifestly not the aim of the present drug movement. Its aim is to induce a trip into an inner world and to forget about society, the family, and work. That this is true of many drug users can be demonstrated by any casual contact with a drug community such as Greenwich Village. There one will meet the drop-outs from society, the run-aways from homes, and the panhandlers.

Furthermore, drug abuse has caused, in some cases, permanent mental illness. And in nearly all drug experiences, there is a type of mental illness which can be psychologically termed as "temporarily induced schizophrenia." Some drug users not only admit that certain drugs have produced in them temporary insanity, but they boast in this fact and have used this insanity as a goal for taking drugs![2]

With this basic understanding of the differences between the medical use and the abusive use of drugs, we can now put forth our thesis:

The use of any drug for the purposes of entertainment, escape, mind control, religious worship, occult experiences, magic, or murder is a sin against God, His Creation, society and the individual.

This thesis condemns any nonmedical use of drugs, regardless if that use has developed into a psychological or physical dependence due to either continuous or infrequent consumption.

Chapter 6

WHAT THE BIBLE SAYS ABOUT DRUGS

Some people say that the Bible does not speak concerning the drug problem. They have come to this conclusion from two basic misunderstandings. They assume that the abuse of drugs is a peculiar twentieth-century phenomenon. Thus, the Bible could not deal with this problem because it was written in ancient times. However, this assumption is not correct. The Ancient World during biblical times was, in fact, filled with drug cultures. The empires and countries surrounding Israel made wide use of drugs as an integral part of their cultural and cultic life.[1]

As to the Jewish awareness of the use of drugs, Genesis 30:14-24 records an episode in which Jacob's wife obtained a love potion called "mandrakes" to cure her barrenness. She soon discovered by bitter failure that only God can open the womb.

The New Testament times witnessed a worse drug problem than we are now experiencing in the twentieth century. For example, drugs played a major part in the popular mystery religions of the first century A.D. There may be an indication of this recorded in Acts 19:18-20, where the people whom Paul had converted turned away from their mystery religion and burned their occult books, which, no doubt, contained recipes for various drugs.[2] With these factors clearly in mind, we can see that the biblical writers were very much aware of the problem of drug abuse.

The second reason some people assume that the Bible does not speak concerning drug abuse is that they have failed to note any place where the biblical writers raise the issue and deal with it. But the Bible does make explicit reference to drug abuse. The reason we cannot see these references is that the English versions of the Bible have obscured these texts by carrying on sixteenth-and-seventeenth century terminology. We are thus faced with the need to define certain terminology before we deal with the biblical texts.

Our English words *pharmacy*, *pharmaceutical*, and *pharmacist* come from one Greek word: *pharmakos*. The etymology of this word refers to the making and use of drugs: "The word means in the classical writers, a preparer of drugs."[3]

Today we view the local pharmacist as the

one who dispenses drugs and the place of distribution as a drugstore. But in biblical times, the one who prepared drugs was the local sorcerer or witch.[4]

Since the preparation and administration of drugs was under the supervision of sorcerers, the word *pharmakos* came to be connected with the art of sorcery and magic.[5] Thus drugs were used for medicine, poison, entertainment, escape, mind control, the occult, religious experience, love potions, and spells. This was the age when men thought they could control the world and manipulate the gods. This was the age of magic, and drugs played a major part in that era. They were the means and the tools by which man attempted to play God and create his own world.[6]

What is now interesting is that Western man is a resurgence of the magical elements of sorcery, witchcraft, the occult, astrology, and Satanism.[7] There is an acknowledged attitude toward drug abuse which views it as a magical solution to personal problems.[8]

With these things in mind, it is astounding to find the Greek word *pharmakos* in the Greek New Testament and in the Greek version of the Old Testament. The occurrences of the word *pharmakos* in the Bible not only link us to the age of magic but to the present-day resurgence of magic. It links us to the use of drugs in the ancient world and in the present age. Wherever the Bible mentions sorcery, it also refers to drug abuse, which was an integral part of ancient sorcery. So when the biblical authors condemn sorcery, their condemnation includes drug abuse.[9] In fact, many well-known New Testament scholars believe the biblical references to sorcery are to be understood as referring to drug abuse. Let us now examine every New Testament reference that uses the Greek word *pharmakos*.

> Walk by the Spirit, and you will not carry out the desire of the flesh. For the flesh sets its desire against the Spirit, and the Spirit against the flesh; for these are in opposition to one another, so that you may not do the things that you please. But if you are led by the Spirit, you are not under the Law. Now the deeds of the flesh are evident, which are: immorality, impurity, sensuality, idolatry, <u>sorcery</u> [Greek *pharmakos*], enmities, strife, jealousy, outbursts of anger, disputes, dissensions, factions, envying, drunkenness, carousing, and things like these, of which I forewarn you just as I have forewarned you that those who practice such things shall not inherit the kingdom of God.

The key word in the text is "sorcery." The English versions translated *pharmakos* as "sorcery" because drugs were a part of the ancient art of sorcery. Even though *pharmakos* was only a part of sorcery, remember, "it literally means the act of administering drugs."[10] In the context of Galatians, *pharmakos* refers to a sin. It has reference to the practice of sorcery and includes drug abuse.[11]

Several observations arise from this passage. According to verse 16 the motivating force behind sorcery (which includes its nonmedicinal use of drugs) is "the desire of the flesh," i.e., the carnal desires of the depraved nature of man. There may be many secondary motives behind taking drugs, such as boredom, kicks, or escape, but the ultimate motive is a self-satisfaction of the inner, depraved desires. This reveals that a drug experience is essentially selfish because it directs one entirely into one's self. Leary's "Hedonic Psychology" is a prime example of this selfish view of life.

Verse 17 describes sorcery as being in total opposition to the work of the Holy Spirit. This is true because sorcery is essentially a deed "of the flesh" (v. 19). And they "who practice such things shall not inherit the kingdom of God" (v.21).

Within the context, the only remedy against sorcery and drug abuse is the work of the Spirit, which places in the believer "love, joy, peace, patience, kindness, goodness, faithfulness, gentleness, self-control" (vv. 22, 23). The work of the Spirit so satisfies the believer that sinful practices lose their appeal.

Also, notice that *pharmakos* appears in the

context of certain other sins. For example, the list "couples idolatry with its habitual ally sorcery."[12] The Scriptures seem to place certain sins together because of an underlying unity. Sorcery and idolatry

> are so frequently found together in the New Testament . . . as to suggest a more intimate connection than the simple fact that sensual excesses usually accompanied idolatrous worship. This fact must be regarded as an indication of some underlying affinity.[13]

With this added insight, let us examine the kinds of sins which are, in some way, generally connected with sorcery and drug abuse.

The list of sinful practices mentioned from verses 19 to 21 falls into four basic categories.[14] To further clarify the different kinds of sins, let's look at the King James text, and then define the words with terms that are used today.

First, there are the sins of sensual passion. "Fornication" refers to premarital sex and to sexual immorality in general. "Uncleanness" refers to unnatural sexual acts such as homosexuality. "Lasciviousness" refers to the giving up of oneself totally to sensuality and is expressed in such sins as pornography and exhibitionist nudity. These are sins against the body.

The second class of sins refers to unlawful dealings in spiritual things. "Idolatry" is the deification of some aspect of created reality. The wood or stone idol of the heathen and the rationalism of a twentieth-century man are both forms of idolatry and are direct sins against God.

The third class encompasses violations of brotherly love or sins against one's neighbor. "Envyings and murders" are included in this category.

The fourth class of sins refers to intemperate excesses or sins against society. They refer to sins which are usually communal and destructive. Such sins as drunkenness and revellings (orgies) are mentioned in the text.

It must be granted that these four kinds of sins seem to accompany a rise in sorcery and drug abuse. Many drug communities are noted for these problems. One could speak of *Oh! Calcutta!* and other manifestations in the counterculture which support the idea of an underlying unity between sorcery (drug abuse) and the rest of the sins in the list.

In Revelation 9:20-21 (KJV) we read,

> The rest of the men which were not
> killed by these plagues yet repented
> not of the works of their hands, that
> they should not worship devils, and
> idols of gold, and silver, and brass,
> and stone, and of wood . . . neither
> repented they of their murders, nor

of their *sorceries* [Greek *pharmak-os*], nor of their fornication, nor of their thefts.

Even after one-third of mankind had perished under the severest punishments of God, man still would not repent of his sins and turn to God for salvation. In describing the hardness of man's heart, John lists certain iniquities which reveal the prominent sins of that age and society. One writer notes, "Among those prominent sins which were listed is the sin of sorcery, i.e., 'lit. drugs.' "[15]

Even the judgment of God could not break man of his addiction to drugs. Only the grace of God can change the heart of a drug-abuser.

Notice once again the sins which accompany drug abuse: They "repented not . . . that they should not worship devils." The worship of Satan and his demons and the rise of witchcraft, astrology, magic, and the occult all seem to be united with a rise in drug abuse.[16] As in Galatians 5, the Bible places the sin of drug abuse in this broader context. The existence of these problems in Eastern societies and their present rise in the counterculture tends to support the idea that there is an underlying unity between these kinds of iniquities. What binds them together is a lust to substitute the world of the creature for the world of the Creator. In his rebellion, man wants to be his own Creator and to live in a world which panders to the desires of the flesh.

They "repented not . . . that they should not worship . . . idols." Having noted the intercoherence of idolatry and drugs, we can see this powerful communion being manifested in the present union of Eastern idolatry and paganism with the American drug-orientated counterculture. Young people are now interested in buying and worshipping idols of Eastern gods such as Krishna. The counterculture is moving in the direction of sheer pagan idolatry. It is this subculture which is the drug-culture.

"Neither repented they of their murders." We are seeing murders everywhere today. Many murders are committed by people who need drugs or because they are on drugs. We see cases of suicide among drug users on a bad trip. There is the murder of children who are given drugs and the murder and deformation of the unborn babies of drug users. We see the murder of a society and a culture, the murder of the minds and rationality of a generation of young people. The apostle did well in placing murder as a sin which accompanies drug abuse.

"Neither repented they of their. . fornication." Someone is bound to ask, "What does drug abuse have to do with sex?" Alan Watts pointed out that drugs cause a person to loosen up in the area of interphysical and intersexual contact with other people.[17] Sometimes certain drugs cause a heightening of sexual sensations during intercourse. When a person takes drugs, he loses self-control, which includes loss of sex-control. Some drug users find themselves doing things which they would not do if they were not high.

"Neither repented they of their . . . thefts." That thievery will plague a drug-ridden community is inevitable. This may be done by an individual drug addict who steals a T.V. or by a pothead who panhandles the public. When you consider that many drug users do not work regularly because of their being high most of the time and that drugs are expensive, one reaches the conclusion that thievery or prostitution is the only way for drug abusers to procure their drugs.

Next let's read Revelation 18:23 (KJV):

> And the light of a candle shall shine no more at all in thee; and the voice of the bridegroom and of the bride shall be heard no more at all in thee: for thy merchants were the great men of the earth; for by thy sorceries [Greek *pharmakos*] were all nations deceived.

Babylon the Great Harlot is destroyed. She is destroyed by divine judgments. In the list of her crimes we can see the root of her power of deception revealed: it is said that by her use of sorcery she deceived the nations. Though highly figurative language must not be interpreted too literally, the idea is that sorcery makes deception possible. Also, sorcerers used drugs to cast their spells in order to deceive people. However, whether we take Revelation 18:23 literally or figuratively, clearly a control and deception over the nations is maintained by the power of sorcery, i.e., drugs.[18]

The use of drugs by a world power in order to control people sounds familiar to modern man. Timothy Leary and Aldous Huxley have proclaimed that the religion of tomorrow will revolve around the drug experience. Drugs will be the sacraments of the new church. In fact, Leary has already formed a church where the use of drugs is prescribed.[19] Other such groups are forming throughout the country.

Moreover, we must see that the governments of this world are not ignorant of the effectiveness of a drugged populace. Some government officials have already suggested that in case of a city-wide riot, a massive amount of tranquilizers should be poured into the water supply to pacify the populace. There have also been occasions where school officials have administered tranquilizers to disorderly students. In light of those possibilities, one Christian leader has said that the invention needed most today is an apparatus which will purify the water coming out of the taps in the home. Such a device could save us and our children from chemical control, for the world powers now have on hand the means for the total manipulation of their people.

The Greek word *pharmakos* appears again in
Revelation 21:8 and 22:15 (KJV):

> The fearful, and unbelieving, and
> the abominable, and murderers, and
> whoremongers, and *sorcerers* [Greek
> *pharmakos*], and idolaters, and all
> liars, shall have their part in the lake
> which burneth with fire and brim-
> stone: which is the second death...For
> outside are dogs, and *sorcerers* [Greek
> *pharmakos*], and whoremongers, and
> murderers, and idolaters, and whoso-
> ever loveth and maketh a lie.

The fate of those who practice sorcery and
drug abuse is described in both passages. Revelation 21:8 describes the judgment of being
cast into the lake of fire, while Revelation
22:15 describes the judgment of being separat-
ed from God and heaven. That God considers
sorcery a serious sin is seen from the gravity of
the other sins in the list and the severity of his
eternal punishment for such practices. It is
interesting to note that the last chapter of the
last book of the New Testament ends with a
warning to those who traffic in sorcery and the
wrong use of drugs.

The New Testament is not alone in coming
out clearly against sorcery and drug abuse. The
Old Testament, the background from which the
New Testament was written, is equally adamant

against drugs for invalid purposes. Examine some of the following places where the word *pharmakos* appears and it will be clear that the Old Testament makes exactly the same points about sorcery that the New Testament does (Exodus 7:11,22; 8:18; 22:18; Deuteronomy 18:11; 2 Kings 9:22; Isaiah 47:9,12; Daniel 2:2; Micah 5:12; Nahum 3:4; Malachi 3:5).

The early church felt Scripture's force against sorcery to be so strong that they met at the Council of Ancyra in Galatia about A.D. 315 to pass a severe canon against all *pharmakos*.[20] The church of today must stand by this historic canon in condemning all forms of sorcery, including drug abuse, which is at present over-running our society. The early Christians saw clearly that drug-cultures and drug-religions are diametrically opposed to biblical Christianity. The truth of this absolute antithesis must be revived in our day so that the church may not only survive but also triumph.

Chapter 7

DRUGS AND GOD

Now that we have examined some of the biblical references to drug abuse, we will consider several theological considerations against it and the drug experience. The first theological consideration is the relationship between God and drug abuse.

The twentieth century is witnessing the rise of drug-centered religious movements. Some of the leaders of this movement are unashamed and, in fact, quite vocal about the religious and mystical experience obtained through the use of drugs. Timothy Leary and Alan Watts constantly refer to the religious and mystical experience gained through the use of LSD and other drugs as a wonderful motive for taking drugs.[1]

Thus we are faced with many people who tie together drugs and God. They may sincerely believe in a "god" which they feel they have experienced or they may be like Aldous Huxley, who did not believe in a god but still liked the "religious" experience of taking drugs.[2]

How has it come about that drugs and God are tied together in the minds of some Western men?

Without a doubt, the rise of Liberalism, Neo-orthodoxy, and the modern theologies during the last one hundred years prepared Western man for drugs.[3] With the rejection of the inspiration and infallibility of the Bible, these theologies had nothing in the realm of "religious experience" to offer people. They did not teach the fear of God or the need for regeneration. They denied the biblical view of salvation and thus left their people with nothing but a dead, formal, and external religion. This created a vacuum within man which drugs now attempt to fill.[4] Liberalism, Neo-orthodoxy, and modern theologies prepared men for drugs by rejecting the real historical Christ and His experiential salvation, which are revealed to us in the Bible. However, this is not the only way in which unorthodox and non-evangelical religions have contributed to the present drug religion.

With the liberal takeover of the major denominations and seminaries, modern theologians have been able to produce their speculative theologies unchecked by any church discipline. Many far-out theologies, such as the "God is Dead" theology, reveal the mass confusion in liberal circles. Yet, within the manifold diversity of modern theology there is an underlying unity. These factions all reject the Christianity of the Scriptures and have substituted in its place a nonrational mentality that views the Bible in terms of an Alice-in-Wonderland salvation-history. They have cut religion free from historical and scientific facts and have interpreted religion as a nonrational leap or state of mind. They have not talked of religious experience in terms of the biblical salvation which involves repentance and conversion, but have stated that a true religious experience is essentially nonrational; i.e., it cannot be talked about or described in terms of the rational categories of normal thought. Thus a religious experience, to them, means an escape from reality and reason. This view of religious experience is not only presented in modern theologies, but also in the modern philosophies, art, music, and literature of the twentieth century.

When this view of religious experience became popular in the Western world, it did not take long for someone to ask, "Why not have such an experience when and where you want it? Why waste time meditating or praying when you can drop acid and have it immediately?" Some liberal, neo-orthodox, and modern theologians have been embarrassed by these questions because of their inability to answer in the negative, while others have jumped on the wagon and recommend the taking of drugs for a religious experience.

But how are modern theologians going to

interpret these drug-induced, nonrational religious experiences when there is nothing like this in biblical Christianity? The answer has come from the East. Since some of the Eastern religions and cultures have used drugs for millennia, they have developed their own religious terminology and concepts by which to interpret this type of experience. Thus we see the wholesale importing of Eastern religious terminology and ideas into Western theology in order not only to explain drug experiences but also to provide a philosophical and religious basis for taking drugs. This influx of Eastern religions has further influenced the rise of drug-induced religious experiences in America.[5]

Biblical Christians reject the modern theological concept of drug-related religious experiences and the Eastern interpretations of such experiences. Both are derived from non-Christian presuppositions that are part of a totally nonbiblical world view. The Bible teaches us that a drug-induced mystical experience is *not* acceptable before God.

However, some people say in objection, "I know that I experienced God through drugs. I met Jesus Christ. God is inside me" or, "I am God." To these statements we answer that we are not denying that there was a spiritual experience, but we do deny the interpretation and evaluation of that experience. We do this on biblical grounds.

There is but one true God who has revealed in

the Holy Scriptures the only Way to Him. The Bible condemns as idolatry all other gods and religions. The way of drugs is a way that may seem right to man, but its ends are the ways of death (Proverbs 16:25).

Let us examine some of the biblical objections to a drug-induced religious experience: "Without faith it is impossible to please Him, for he who comes to God must believe that He is" (Hebrews 11:6). The way to God is the way of faith. The Bible clearly defines *faith* as "that certain conscious commitment of the whole man to the Lord Jesus Christ in all the glory of His person and work." Faith is that gift of God which enables sinners rationally, volitionally, and emotionally to submit to Jesus Christ and trust in Him for forgiveness of their sins and ultimate salvation. "God is spirit, and those who worship Him must worship in spirit and truth" (John 4:24). The true worship of God requires that "you shall love the Lord your God with *all* your *heart*, and with *all* your *soul*, and with *all* your *mind*, and with *all* your *strength*" (Mark 12:30). God accepts only the worship that comes from the entire man in all his conscious faculties, for "the Father seeketh such to worship him" (John 4:23 KJV).

During a drug-induced experience a person cannot really believe, love, obey, or worship the true God. With his heart gone, his soul high, his mind blown, and his strength evaporated, he cannot worship God. The true way of worshiping God requires the conscious commitment and exercise of the entire conscious faculties of the whole man. Man renders himself incapable of worshipping the true God when he takes drugs.

A drug-induced experience has the opposite effect of the experience of conversion to Christ. The Scriptures clearly show that the effect of Christ's redemption upon a person is the opposite effect that drugs have on a person. When Christ healed and saved the demonic man named Legion, the Bible says that the townspeople found "the man who had been demon-possessed sitting down, clothed and *in his right mind*" (Mark 5:15). Christ had brought Legion into a state of conscious sanity and normality. Also, Jesus pictured the first step in the conversion of the prodigal son as "*he came to his senses*" (Luke 15:17). The work of the Spirit produces a "sound mind" in the believer (2 Timothy 1:7 KJV). St. Luke in Acts 19:18-20 represents the sign of conversion as a turning away from all forms of sorcery.

Throughout the Bible, salvation is seen as the work of Christ in restoring men to a state of sanity and normality because all men are insanely attempting to escape from God (Romans 1, 2). However, a drug experience would put Legion out of his right mind and have the prodigal son "leaving his senses." Thus the drug experience is diametrically opposed to the salvation which is found in the Lord Jesus Christ.

Drugs are actually used by many as a way to get to God without going through Jesus Christ.

They are ignoring that Jesus said, "I am the way, and the truth, and the life; no one comes to the Father, but through Me" (John 14:6). And, "There is . . . one mediator also between God and men, the man Christ Jesus" (1 Timothy 2:5). The drug user attempts to substitute his drugs for conscious faith in Jesus Christ. His drugs are his mediator. His chemicals become his saviour, redeemer, and god. And the use of drugs is conducive to forms of idolatry such as pantheism or self-deification. Just as God condemned the tower of Babel, so does God condemn the modern chemical tower of Babel.

A drug-induced experience is opposed not only to the worship of the Father and the redemption of the Son but also to the work of the Holy Spirit. Since the Fall, man has attempted to find inward peace, happiness, and joy by any means except the way laid out for him by God in the Scriptures. Man has tried pagan religions, meditation, psychology, formalism, and now drugs. But drugs do not produce true love, joy, and peace because these are the fruits of the Holy Spirit (Galatians 5:16-23).

It is true that God, in His infinite grace, may save a man in spite of his alcoholism or drug abuse. But it is equally true that God never saves a man through chemicals. Salvation is attainable only by that conscious faith and commitment of the whole man to the Lord Jesus Christ.

Let it also be pointed out that a person may have a religious experience with some super-

natural being, such as a demon, through the use
of drugs. But he can never get to God by any
other means than faith in Christ, for "there is
salvation in no one else; for there is no other
name under heaven that has been given among
men, by which we must be saved" (Acts 4:12).

Chapter 8

DRUGS AND THE EARTH

The Scriptures begin with a description of the creation of the heavens and the earth. Upon creating the earth, God prepared it for the coming of man—the crown and glory of the creation of God. Man was made in the image and likeness of God. Only on the basis of this truth can we distinguish man from the animal and the machine. He alone bears the image of God.

God then gave man certain duties and responsibilities to perform. Man was not created to lie down and do nothing. His creation was unto a particular function in this world. What was this work for which man was created?

"And God blessed them; and God said to them, 'Be fruitful and multiply, and fill the earth, and subdue it; and rule over the fish of the sea and over the birds of the sky, and over every living thing that moves on the earth'" (Genesis 1:28). In these words we find the original cultural mandate wherein God called man to cultivate and to develop the earth to the glory of God. God assigns man two duties by which to teach him how his responsibility to develop the earth's potentials can be fulfilled.

"God took the man and put him into the garden of Eden to cultivate it and keep it" (Genesis 2:15). In this duty man exercised his dominion over the soil and the plants. He was to keep and care tenderly for the garden and not to exploit it.

"And the man gave names to all the cattle, and to the birds of the sky, and to every beast of the field" (Genesis 2:20). As the keeping of the garden expressed man's duty to labor physically in developing the world, so the naming of the animals expressed man's duty to labor intellectually in understanding the world. Here we have the biblical basis for the enterprise of science. In fact, biblical Christianity is the only valid basis for science.[1]

However, man fell into sin and rebellion. After the Fall, man no longer liked physical and intellectual labor. Man began to exploit and destroy the earth instead of tending and keeping it. Rather than working as God intended, some men began to force others to work for them or to exploit and steal from the weak. In this way man neglected and abused the cultural mandate.

Drug abuse is a form of rejecting the cultural mandate. When a person is high, he usually is not concerned with physical or intellectual duties. He is not concerned with work or the need to develop the earth.[2] In fact, drugs render him incapable of keeping the cultural mandate. In this he sins against the earth.

Why does drug abuse violate the cultural mandate? Drugs are an escape into an inner world where there is no sense of responsibility to function. It is not surprising that a growing number of young drug users have no interest in the sciences. Drugs turn people inward to themselves while the sciences point outward to the earth.

Drugs may also blind people to the evil and disharmony in the world. Because they see nothing but so-called beauty and harmony when high, they tend to think that the real world is an illusion and their drug-produced hallucination is the real world. Marijuana is particularly guilty in this area. It cuts down on people's motivation to do physical and mental labor. While they are high on pot, the earth can go to "pot" for all they care.[3]

For man to obey the cultural mandate, he needs all his faculties geared to a conscious working with the creation. The indiscriminate use of drugs tends to negate the cultural mandate and cause man to cease working in the function for which he was created. Drug abuse, then, is a sin against the earth.

Chapter 9

DRUGS AND SOCIETY

Human society is not the chance product of blind evolution. Its origin and formation go back to the creation of mankind. Adam and Eve formed the first human society.

There are some who would teach us that human society is ultimately meaningless and has no real significance. Community, love, and the structures of family, school, church, and state are regarded as temporary expressions of man's onward evolution. Human society appeared and will disappear without giving any real meaning or significance for its existence.

But the Bible places human society in the light of the divine society. Man in community reflects the Triune God in community. From all eternity the Triune God existed in a community of love, communication, and shared life. That human society is a parallel puts it in its proper light and gives it meaning and significance.[1]

Thus what a man does in or to human society really matters. A widespread turning to drugs has always been detrimental to a society. The effects of the popular use of certain drugs on a society have been apparent in some Eastern countries. It would be beneficial if the leaders of our counterculture realized what a popular use of drugs could do to us. One such leader, Andrew Weil, has admitted that, "clearly much drug taking in our country is negative in the sense that it is ultimately destructive to the individual and therefore to society."[2]

When Jesus said that we were to love God with all our heart, soul, mind, and strength, He added, "thou shalt love thy neighbor as thyself" (Mark 12:31 KJV). Someone under the influence of drugs cannot truly "love" his neighbor in the biblical sense of love. That biblical love is described well in 1 Corinthians 13. Biblical love is a conscious responsible activity of man toward God and his neighbor. It requires the functioning of the whole man. Drug abuse renders a person incapable of this type of love.

Some people have rebelled at this and said, "Well, I know that when I am high I love everybody. The love which I have during a high is fantastic and unbelievable. And you should feel what it is like to make love when high. Man, that's love!" It is evident that this person confuses fleshly excitement and lust for love. Since, according to Leary and Watts, the subject-object relationship disappears during a drug experience, it follows that all true interpersonal relationships disappear.[3] Consequently, true love is impossible during a drug experience.

Other social problems arise from drug abuse. We have already seen how the Bible places drug abuse among a host of social evils such as murder and theft. One trip through a drug community will show filth, poverty, crime, disease, and immorality. Drug abusers are usually a negative force in any society.

It is also apparent that a widespread, popular use of drugs produces many people who simply "drop out" of society. They do not produce for society but live off of it by stealing, going on welfare, becoming prostitutes, or panhandling.

A drug user dropout may say, "I do not hurt anyone. I just do my own thing." But he is wrong. All people who are social or economic dropouts are hurting society. When a society has absorbed too many dropouts, it is then forced to destroy them or be destroyed. A great fear exists that our society will be forced into the extreme right or left politically in order to control the drug-culture dropouts. Whether this happens or not, the popular use of drugs is not good for any society.[4]

Chapter 10

DRUGS AND
THE INDIVIDUAL

Now that we have examined drug abuse in relation to God, the earth, and society, we should look at it in relation to the individual. Because this matter is personal by its very nature, it is necessary for each one to think through seriously why he should not take drugs.

God created man to bear His image. One of the clear attributes of God is His self-control or self-sovereignty, which is accompanied by His immutability. God never "blows His mind" or goes on a "trip."

We can know that by looking at the Lord Jesus Christ, who perfectly revealed the Father to us. "No man has seen God at any time; the only begotten [Son], who is in the bosom of the Father, He has explained Him" (John 1:18). His life is the purest example of sanity and conscious self-control. In contrast, when man enters into a drug-induced state, he loses his

67

self-control and submits to the rule of the drug. He may decide to take the drug, but once he has taken it, he does not have any control over the length or effect of his drug experience. He cannot decide to have a good trip rather than a bad trip.

The Bible condemns gluttony and drunkenness, because both cause loss of self-control. In these sins, food and alcohol control the consumer. Whoremongers also lose self-control and are under the rule of their sex drive. In this way, drug abuse destroys an aspect of the image of God in man. It destroys a part of man's humanity and dignity.

The destruction of the image of God in man is carried out in other ways than the loss of self-control. Man's rationality is temporarily laid aside while he is high. Drugs warp man's sense of time and history. They twist his perception of the real world. They sometimes render him incapable of communicating coherently to others. In many instances, during a drug experience one loses the sense of being an individual person distinct from everything else. This destroys the image of God in man and thus reduces man to the level of an animal, a plant, or a machine.

Something else which is usually lost during a drug experience is one's sense of being a mere creature. Drugs seem to create a sense of euphoria which expresses itself as power to transcend all "creatureliness." One feels that he has transcended time and space and has become a god.

It is this state of euphoria which has led some to think of themselves as a god or a superman who can fly—and leap to their death from tall buildings.[1]

It is interesting to note that Satan's main temptation to man at the Fall was "you will be like God" (Geneses 3:5). Ever since the Fall, man has tried to experience godhood. Certain drugs offer this experience. For example, God is above time. Drugs can make one think he has transcended time. God is infinite. Drugs may make a person feel he is infinite. In many users, drugs create a period of self-deification which eventually causes great psychological problems and possible physical harm.

As an individual, one must be prepared to suffer physically from some drugs. Do not be fooled; Speed kills. LSD probably breaks chromosomes.[2] Many drugs destroy brain cells. In several recent studies marijuana has been shown to have adverse effects.* Even if one finds a drug which at the present has no known physical side-effect, the chances of physical injury by an accident during a drug experience are great. A person's sense of pain can be destroyed. Thus, some people have bled to death because they did not know that they were cut.

The Bible is clear that the body of a Christian is the temple of the Holy Spirit and is not to be harmed in any way. "Or do you not know that

---

* See Appendix A.

your body is a temple of the Holy Spirit who is in you, whom you have from God, and that you are not your own?" (1 Corinthians 6:19).

There are always grave psychological dangers involved in drug use. Drugs can destroy or permanently alter the mind of man. When one starts on drugs, he must expect basic and permanent changes in his personality.

One example is the "child mentality" encountered throughout the drug culture. Some have taken drugs so often that even when they are off drugs they act as if they are still high. Their speech is strictly stream-of-consciousness. Many times they have lost the ability to concentrate or read. At all times they assume an innocent, childlike character. By this means they escape the world of responsible adults. The motivation for any physical or mental labor is gone.

Not only can drugs destroy the image of God, the body, and the mind, but they can also stunt the growth of an individual's character. People use tranquilizers to escape from the pain, stress, and suffering involved in living in the real world.

The use of tranquilizers is more popular today than ever before in the history of drug abuse. One of the possible reasons is that we are living in an "Instant Age." All our foods and commodities can be prepared instantly. Thus people become inclined to demand an instant release from stress and strain.[3] So they turn to tranquilizers which produce a sense of euphoria by which they escape their problems instantly.

It is a great shame but it is true that even people who attend church are using tranquilizers. Maybe this is why many young people do not listen to adults. Drug users point out the hypocrisy of some professing Christians. Those who use tranquilizers condemn young drug users for tuning in and getting high, when they themselves are using drugs to tune down and turn off!

James 1:2-4 states that suffering and tribulation are God's way of enabling a person to grow in grace. However, taking pills is much easier than pursuing biblical sanctification. Some people think, "Why spend hours in prayer when a pill can give me instant peace? Why seek to mortify the sin of anxiety when a tranquilizer can calm my nerves?" But if a person takes a tranquilizer every time he faces tribulation or suffering, and thus chemically obliterates the situation from his mind, how can he grow? If he never seems to develop the grace of patience, it may be because he never allows himself to have the "mother" of patience: tribulation.

The use of drugs also opens the individual to demonic and satanic control. Some ancient Eastern religions and the early American Indian religions used drugs in their occult worship. And many pagan religions today use drugs to gain entrance into the spirit world to commune with evil spirits and gods.

We do not deny the experience of meeting and worshipping spiritual beings while on drugs. However, the apostle Paul warns us that the

pagans are dealing with demons and evil spirits
(1 Corinthians 10:20). To come under the control of Satan is a fearful price to pay for a drug
experience.

There is one other lesson which is very clear:
Addiction means slavery. When we are physically or mentally addicted to a plant, drink, or
drug, then it has mastered us. It controls us. We
live and move according to its dictates. The
apostle Paul's statement in 1 Corinthians 6:12 is
very apropos at this point: "I will not be mastered by anything." Within the context, he is
asserting the truth that a person should not be
controlled by an inordinate desire for food (v.
13) or immorality (vv. 15-18). He makes his
body his servant, not his master (1 Corinthians
9:27). To be mastered by food is gluttony, by sex
is whoremongery, by alcohol is drunkenness,
and by drugs is addiction or habituation. The
Christian must aim to not be mastered by or
addicted to anything.

Lastly, a person does not need to turn to drugs
as a way of life and fulfillment. Jesus Christ
stands before all men in the free offer of the
gospel. His salvation is the only true fulfilling
way of life, for "ye are complete in Him" (Colossians 2:10 KJV). As long as we stand outside His
grace, we are under the wrath of God. All our
plans and methods for peace and joy in this world
or in the psychedelic world of drugs will avail
nothing in this life or on the Day of Divine Judgment. The gospel calls us to repent from our sins
and turn to Jesus Christ for salvation.

Chapter 11

PARENTS, PASTORS, AND TEACHERS

There are two methods of stopping an epidemic. One is to give a preventative medicine to inoculate people against the disease. The other is to treat people after they have the disease. It is obvious that preventative medicine is a better and wiser path to follow when dealing with an epidemic.

We are now faced with an epidemic of drug abuse, particularly among young people. Drug abuse runs rampant among university students, high-school students, is becoming popular among junior-high-school students, and is even growing among elementary-school children.

But what about children from Christian homes? Steve Arterburn and Jim Burns have pointed out that they drink almost as much as unchurched kids, and actually use more marijuana.[1] So Christian parents, pastors, and teachers must be prepared to deal with drug abuse whether it appears in the home, the church, or the school.

The first preventative aid against drug abuse is an informed Christian home where the biblical norms are put into practice. The father, mother, and child should accept their respective roles within the biblical structure of the family (Ephesians 5:22-25,28,29,33; 6:1-4). The parents should constantly teach their children biblical precepts (Ephesians 6:4). They should establish a consistent family worship. They should unashamedly practice true biblical discipline (Ephesians 6:4; Proverbs 23:13,14). Parents should seek to educate their children about the temptations to drug abuse which they will eventually face on the street or in school. They must warn them of the dangers to themselves and others. We have the biblical example of Solomon warning his sons against the temptations of his day (Proverbs 2:1) Parents also must be careful that they themselves are not abusing any drug, alcohol, tobacco, or tranquilizer. In everything they should have a biblically structured home life. For further information we recommend the audio tape series "Christian Parenting."[1]

A biblically structured church life is another important preventative aid against drug abuse. There should be a powerful, consistent, expository preaching of the whole counsel of God. Pointed applications should be made to all present, including the young people and children (Acts 20:26,27). The problem of drug abuse should be presented and discussed in the worship service and in youth meetings. Pastors should present the biblical perspective on drug abuse to their young people. They should arrange for several people who were converted from drug abuse to give their testimonies. Such testimonies have a powerful effect on the young. Pastors must inoculate their people by the powerful preaching of the Word of God against desiring the drug experience.

The Christian school and teacher is a third preventative aid against drug abuse. Not only is a Christian school less likely to harbor drug abusers, but it is also a place where positive Christian instruction can be given (Psalm 1). The Christian teacher can instill the biblical world view into the minds of the students. If students learn to think in biblical terms, they will see through much of the drug-abuse propaganda. While the society around us disintegrates, the Christian school is a very important aid in maintaining a healthy Christian community.

The greatest and most complete preventative aid against drug abuse is personal salvation. If the child, church member, or student is brought to a saving knowledge of the Lord Jesus Christ, there is little likelihood that he will ever be involved in drug abuse. Even if the young person is not converted, the blessings of a Christian home, church, and school will act as a common grace barrier against all gross sin, including drug abuse, for if we "train up a child in the way he should go, even when he is old he will not depart from it" (Proverbs 22:6).

But what positive steps can be taken when drug abuse is not just a possibility but an agonizing reality? What should we do when someone confesses that he is using drugs?

One definite way to be prepared for such a situation, whether it appears in the home, church, or school, is to ground ourselves thoroughly in the biblical principles of counseling. An excellent book which will prove of great help to Christian parents, pastors, and teachers is *Competent to Counsel* by Jay Adams.[3] Dr. Adams gives a concise and lucid presentation of the biblical perspective on counseling. It will help to equip every Christian to give biblical counsel in every area of life.

Christian Parents

1. Don't panic upon discovering drug abuse in the home. Some parents have panicked, lost their tempers, and finally forced their child to leave home. They fail to realize that a child whose home is closed to him will probably become totally dependent upon the drug culture. As long as he remains in the home, he is under his parents' influence and counsel. Remember at all times that the servant of the Lord should not strive but be kind, able to teach, patient, and gentle (2 Timothy 2:23-26). Also, "fathers, do not provoke your children to anger" (Ephesians 6:4).

2. Don't try to counsel someone while he is under the influence of a drug. It will generally be a waste of time. Sometimes he is so depressed that he does not want to listen. Other times he is so high and giddy that he cannot listen. He will often agree or disagree with everything. He cannot discuss the issue in an objective manner. It is better to wait until the influence of drugs has worn off. Then talk to him.

If you're not sure whether your child is ready to talk, look for the tell-tale signs of drug use. While there is no one definite sign to look for because of so many different types of drugs, there is usually something abnormal taking place which you can discern. Check to see whether any physical, mental, or personality abnormalities are manifested before you attempt to discuss the issue. The eyes may be dilated, blank, swollen, and red, or they may be normal, depending on the drug. Your child may be extremely depressed or happy and carefree. His speech may be unusually fast or slow.

3. Don't seek to hide the problem from your pastor and doctor. By hiding the problem, one reveals that he views his name and prestige as being more important than his child. Seek the counsel of others, for in the counsel of the many, there is safety (Proverbs 11:14).

4. Seek patiently and lovingly to communicate to your child that you love and care for him and that this is why you are very much concerned

about his welfare. Let him know that you want to understand and to help him.

5. Seek to secure answers for the questionnaire at the end of the chapter so that you can better understand the problem and also give a fuller explanation of it to others.

6. Be firm that drug abuse is a sin against God, a sin from which he should repent. Don't allow any pantheistic argument for or explanation of his drug experiences to go unchallenged. Give the biblical explanation of the drug experience. Carefully explain the biblical understanding and rejection of drug abuse.

7. Be careful to see that he does not shift his responsibility and blame to someone or something else. Often a person will claim that he could not help himself. Our first parents tried to shift the blame and responsibility from themselves to God and others (Genesis 3:12,13). Just as God confronted them and held them completely responsible, so you must also do the same.

8. Call your pastor and elders to ask for their prayers, guidance, and assistance. Ask about the biblical guidelines to use in dealing with this situation. Set an appointment with the pastor so that he can counsel your child.

9. Call your physician and arrange a complete medical checkup for your child. There may be physical or brain damage. The damage may be due to the drugs themselves or to the method used to take the drug. Perhaps a dirty or infected needle was used for injection. Also learn about

the drugs your child has taken and what the signs and effects of them are. Set up an appointment with the physician to discuss drugs with your child.

10. One of the most difficult duties you as a parent may face in drug abuse is the possible necessity of your being in contact with the police. There are several reasons for having to go to the proper authorities.

First, when the use and possession of certain drugs is illegal, the Christian is under the God-given responsibility to obey the state in these matters (Romans 13:1-8; Titus 3:1; 1 Peter 2:13-17).

Second, your child may have confessed to you that to obtain money for drugs he has been shoplifting, mugging, burglarizing, prostituting, or even making and selling drugs. If you have knowledge of such crimes and seek to hide them, you can be criminally charged as an accomplice to the crimes.

Third, tell your child that he must make as much restitution for his crimes as possible because the Bible views restitution for criminal offenses as an essential part of true spiritual repentance (Exodus 22:1; Leviticus 6:5; Numbers 5:6-8; 2 Samuel 12:6; Luke 19:8,9). If your child is still your responsibility because of his age, you must try to help make restitution as much as possible.

Fourth, you have the responsibility to "love your neighbor as yourself" (Matthew 19:19).

You should contact the parents of any other youths involved in drug abuse. "To one who knows the right thing to do, and does not do it, to him it is sin" (James 4:17). This action could deliver others from addiction. If you discover that drug abuse is going on in your child's school, report this to the proper authorities. They will appreciate any help or information you can give.

Also, seek to have your child tell everything he knows about the drug business in his area. The names of the pushers and manufacturers should be given to the police. They may be able to follow these leads and destroy the drug ring in the area. By this action thousands of parents and children may be delivered from the agony of drug abuse. Of course, guard your personal safety by doing these things with the utmost secrecy. But be obedient to God's law and leave the consequences to Him. If you must suffer for doing right as a Christian, count it all joy for the glory of God (1 Peter 2:12, 19-21; 3:13-17).

Christian Pastors

1. Don't assume that only a psychologist or psychiatrist can deal with the problem. The Scriptures sufficiently equip the man of God for every good work (2 Timothy 3:15-17). Drug abuse is a problem which a pastor is competent to handle because it is, at its roots, a spiritual problem of sin.

2. Don't immediately push for a quick decision. It will more than likely produce a "stony ground" hearer (Matthew 13:20,21). Faith involves knowledge as well as trust and assent. Be careful that the person understands the nature of the help you offer. There may be brain damage to such a degree that he is rendered incapable of believing the gospel. It may be weeks before the mind of a drug abuser clears sufficiently to understand the gospel. Of course, in the initial state of mental confusion during which a person comes for help, it may be easy to have him make a decision. But this type of decision will not ultimately bear the fruits of salvation.

3. Use the basic questionnaire at the end of the chapter. You need to know as much as possible.

4. If the person is underage and still living in his parents' home, contact the parents even if the child pleads for you to keep silent. Christian parents particularly should be involved from the very beginning.

5. Advise the person to get a medical checkup as soon as possible. Be prepared to advise hospitalization if necessary.

6. Most of all, lovingly but firmly confront the person with his sin and press home the gospel call to faith and repentance through the Lord Jesus Christ.

7. Be prepared to deal with the religious theology of Eastern philosophy. One book which gives a good presentation of Eastern philosophy

and its relationship to drug abuse is *Zen-Existentialism* by Dr. Lit-Sen Chang.[4] This book has proven quite effective in a number of cases.

8. Advise the person to sit under the preaching of the Word of God, for it is the power of God to salvation (Romans 1:16; 1 Corinthians 1:18). The local church plays a very important part in the counseling program. It is generally the place of spiritual birth and growth.

Christian School and Teachers

1. As a teacher, you have the opportunity of observing young people every day. You may observe some symptoms of drug abuse in the classroom. If a student is constantly sleeping, tardy, irresponsible, absent, answering incoherently, listless, lacking motivation, or giving any unusual physical sign such as blank, glassy, or dilated eyes, he may be taking drugs. If a student has Band-Aids on the inside of his elbows over a long period of time, he may be on hard drugs. On the other hand, there may be no physical signs of drug abuse. But there is usually some abnormal behavior which you can observe. If a student shows the characteristics of mental retardation and there has been no previous medical history of it, there may be drug abuse. Be alert and be aware of your students.

2. Besides watching for a student who may be taking drugs, be alert to the passing of drugs among students. Also, report any stranger on or

near the campus who is giving or selling things to a student. The drug pusher views the school and university as prime targets.

3. Once drug abuse is discovered in a student, the school authorities, the parents, and the police should be notified. Silence means golden opportunity for the pusher to contact and ensnare more students.

4. Support any antidrug-abuse program in the school. Help to secure good films and speakers who will educate the students about the sinfulness and harmfulness of drug abuse.

These are some of the practical steps to take to prevent and to deal with drug abuse. Every Christian parent, pastor, and teacher should be prepared to deal with the drug abuse problem.

Counselor's Questionnaire For Drug Users

1. Are you intending to stop drugs?
2. Why?
3. Why come to me?
4. Are you high now?
5. When was the last time you took drugs?
6. History:
   a. First time you took a drug:
   b. What was it?
   c. What was the environment?
   d. Where did you get it (from whom)?
   e. Why did you first try it?
   f. Did you have to pay for it?
   g. What other drugs have you used?

        (1) Strength?
        (2) How many times?
  h. Any particular drug on a regular basis?
        (1) What is it?
        (2) How long have you been on it regularly?
        (3) Do you feel that it is physiologically or psychologically addicting?

i.   Do you have any drugs on your person now, at home, or in a cache?

j.   Will you bring them to me right away? Do you promise to not contact a pusher for any more?

k. Are you willing to destroy all the drugs in your possession?

l.   From whom do you get drugs?

m. With whom and where do you usually take it?

n. Are you willing to forsake all individuals, places, and occasions connected with drugs?

7. Drug experience:

Write down each drug you have taken and what you experienced, particularly noting any spiritual or religious experiences; whether you were being taken over by a spiritual or evil personality; whether you ever desired to hurt people or self; any suicidal tendencies and whether you had any bummers, any flashbacks, or sexual activities associated with each drug.

8. Medical history:
   a. What physical effects from drugs have you noticed in yourself?
   b. How have you taken the drugs? Have you ever used a needle?
   c. Are you willing to have a complete medical checkup?

9. Are you willing to go to the pastor for counseling?
10. Are you willing to go to your parents?
11. Where did you get the money to buy drugs?
12. Are you willing to make restitution for any crimes connected with drugs?
13. Are you willing to tell the police all you know about the drug business in your school or area?

Chapter 12

THE GOSPEL
AND THE
DRUG ABUSER

Considerable care must be used in presenting the gospel to drug abusers. Much harm has been done by unbiblical procedures in presenting the gospel. Two basic principles are extremely helpful in witnessing. These principles are not viewed as a self-contained plan of salvation, but rather, as helpful observations concerning witnessing which arise out of the Scriptures and Christian experience.

There is, first of all, the necessity of finding out the motives behind the drug abuser's seeking help. What are his conscious needs? Why does he come for help? What help is he looking for? The importance of these questions is based upon the fact that a person's needs will determine the help and hope for which he seeks. The nature of the need will dictate the nature of the help desired. Thus, without finding out what the person wants, you may not know if he is coming

87

to you for the right reason. For example, if you are unaware that he is seeking salvation for the wrong reasons, you may give him a false answer and deceive him.

False reasons and false answers have led to numerous false decisions. This is one great fault of many forms of modern evangelism. They address themselves to the conscious needs of a man and promise that the gospel has come to satisfy those needs. Emotional appeals are made to persons who are conscious of their need for happiness, friendship, security, and stability. Various intellectual appeals are made to persons who are conscious of their need for philosophical identity, significance, and meaning. Other appeals have promised that Christ will make a person popular, healthy in body and mind, and will help put money in the bank.

While these needs can be real, essential, and important to the person, they in no way satisfy the real needs of a sinner. The gospel spells out the spiritual needs of man, which can be satisfied only in salvation through Christ. Nowhere in the gospels do we find Jesus saying that He came to make people happy, wealthy, and wise. Those may be side effects of salvation, but they do not constitute the purpose of Christ's coming. He came to save sinners who were conscious of their sin and their need of salvation (Matthew 9:13; 11:28, 29).

Here is an illustration you might find helpful: One drug abuser approached us asking for help.

He was obviously very sincere about seeking spiritual help. But we were careful not to ask him for an immediate decision, as many modern evangelicals might have done. We asked him what were the conscious needs which were bringing him to us. He stated that he was in a very confused mental state. Three times he had attempted suicide and had been in the state mental institution. He wanted to know if the gospel promised (1) psychological help in the healing of his mind, (2) spiritual help in getting peace, (3) help in learning to live and work productively in society and with his family, and (4) educational help in learning deeper knowledge and the ability to read better.

All these needs were real to him, and they were the reasons for his coming. But the needs which the Bible indicate as being the conscious basis for faith in Christ for salvation were missing. The man had no conscious awareness of sin, guilt, and hell. He had no concept of the need for salvation through the person and work of Christ.

Upon deeper talks, it was soon clear that he was indoctrinated with the Eastern philosophical concepts of pantheism and reincarnation. There was no proper conceptual framework within which he could understand the gospel. In the weeks to follow, the Eastern concepts were discussed and refuted. Then the biblical world view of Creation, Fall, and Redemption replaced them. These truths helped him discover who he was, where he came from, why he was here, and where he was going.

Soon after he came to understand the gospel. God was gracious to give him a conscious sense of his sin and guilt. He saw his absolute need of personal salvation through Christ, and God was pleased to save him. Had we not asked in the beginning what his needs were, his decision for salvation might not have been genuine.

The second principle is to present the needs of man which the Scriptures reveal as necessary for salvation. Christ did not come to call the righteous, but to call sinners to repentance (Matthew 9:13). When Jesus dealt with the woman at the well, He was careful to reveal her sin and need of forgiveness (John 4:16-18). The outline of the book of Romans reveals the apostle Paul's basic method of presenting the gospel. In chapters 1-3, he reveals the needs of man in terms of God's wrath, man's sin and guilt, and the universality of human depravity. He does not capitalize on the conscious needs of the Gentiles and Jews as being sufficient for salvation. In chapters 4-11, he presents God's rich provision to meet those needs revealed in chapters 1-3. That's because the person and work of Christ cannot be understood apart from an understanding of those needs which make salvation necessary. Until the law of God is known, sin cannot be recognized for what it is (Romans 3:20; 7:7). If sin is not recognized, there is no need or appreciation of the salvation provided by God through Christ to destroy sin and its effects. One book which helps to explain this is *Studies in the Atonement*.[1]

The drug abuser should be asked to explain what his conscious needs and motives are. Then he should be told the nature of his real needs— of which he must be conscious. Explain in some detail the rich provision of God in the gospel. The Lord Jesus Christ, in all His preincarnate glory, was sent by the Father to rescue sinners from His wrath and judgment and to procure eternal redemption for the people of God. The Lord Jesus came to live and die to turn away God's just and holy anger and to provide forgiveness of sin and eternal life. In conscious awareness of his sin and guilt before God, the drug abuser should submit to the Lord Jesus Christ as his Prophet, Priest, and King. He will soon discover that the grace of God is sufficient to meet his every need.

While it is wonderful to see someone accept Jesus Christ as his Lord and Saviour, the daily trials of discipleship have just begun. The drug abuser will generally have special problems and require special care. The temptation to return to drug dependence will sometimes return. Any physical or psychological damage must be gradually corrected. Regular attendance upon the powerful preaching of the Word of God and the community life of the local church will be a most important aid in adjusting the new believer to

the Christian life. Through the appointed means
of grace, the converted drug abuser will soon be
joyously testifying to the satisfying and fulfilling saving grace of God.

CONCLUSION

We have examined drug abuse and the drug experience in the light of the biblical concepts of the Creation, the Fall, and Redemption. We have seen that the Bible condemns the use of drugs for magic, murder, entertainment, mind control, escape, occult experience, religious worship, and all other nonmedical uses. We have investigated the biblical basis for rejecting drug abuse and the drug experience and have found that it is a sin against God, the world, society, and the individual. In all these things we have attempted by God's grace to present what the Bible teaches. Of course, if one rejects the Bible, he will reject the biblical position. In doing so, he rejects God. This is perhaps the real sign of our age. This is a God-rejecting age where man no longer bows in humility before his Maker and heeds His revealed will.

As Christians face this new age of paganism

and drugism, they must not keep silent. The church must now arise to seize the present opportunities. Many young people are open to talk about religion. Some of them are asking the right questions. So let us, by God's grace, give them the biblical answers. In doing so, we may see a great reformation sweep over the Western world once again. We must not despair but arise to the challenge of the age. We must boldly proclaim God's Word to a rebellious and idolatrous generation.

MARIJUANA

A frank discussion on marijuana (often called "pot" or "grass") is greatly needed today. There is much widespread ignorance and mythology concerning this controversial drug. We must be careful to separate fact and fantasy when it comes to marijuana. Since it is an important and relevant subject, it certainly merits a detailed examination.

Two factors make research into the nature and effects of marijuana particularly crucial at this time. First, it is a fact that over eight million people in the United States have probably used this drug at least once. It is common knowledge that vast numbers of college and high-school students are using the drug. Its use has become quite widespread at many colleges, universities, and rock concerts.

Second, there is a strong movement to legalize the use of marijuana. But before we legalize pot and put thousands of high drivers on the road, research must first establish its absolute harmlessness. This has not been done yet.

Marijuana is not a hard narcotic such as opium or heroin. It is not physically addictive and it does not chemically lead to the use of harder drugs. The active ingredient in marijuana is THC (tetrahydrocannabind). In its pure form, THC is a strong hallucinogen with some sedative properties. The amount of THC in marijuana varies considerably. One batch may produce nothing, while another batch will produce a powerful experience equal to an LSD trip. Few medical uses of the drug have been established. It is thought that it may be of use for increasing the appetite of cancer patients and it relieves some of the symptoms of glaucoma but not much else is known at the present.

Marijuana can produce many different sensations. Much depends upon the mental state and expectations of the user, his environment, and the amount and strength of the drug. One interesting point is that frequent users increasingly need less of the drug to get high. This curious fact is not completely understood at the present.

The effect of marijuana on the mind has been compared by many to the effect of such mind-expanding drugs as LSD, speed, or mescaline. And there are significant effects common to all these drugs. But it should be pointed out that marijuana is not as strong as other hallucinogens and generally does not produce vivid hallucinations.

Recent research has established the general or common sensations which make up a marijuana-type drug experience:

1. There is a distortion and heightening of one's sensual perception of the world. A person's abilities too see, hear, taste, touch, and smell are generally confused and distorted. Thus many users find exceptional pleasure in eating spicy food, hearing music, or having sex.

2. A temporal disintegration is experienced by the user. Time can seem to slow down, speed up, or even stop. When high, the user is conscious only of the present and its sensations. The past and the future are completely forgotten.

3. It is thought by many that this temporal disintegration causes the amotivational syndrome so characteristic of marijuana users. Even those who are pro-marijuana admit that there is a correspondence between the use of marijuana and mental indifference, laziness, and lack of goal-centeredness. The present sensual pleasures completely captivate the attention of the user.

4. The ability to judge distances correctly is distorted by marijuana. Research has shown that many marijuana users misjudge distances. Driving tests have demonstrated that infrequent and light users of marijuana cannot drive a car properly. Some heavy users of marijuana have learned over a period of time to compensate for distance distortion. But they still rank below normal in their automatic reflexes. These facts

are particularly important when we consider whether to legalize the use of marijuana.

5. Mental functions are impaired by marijuana. Recent research by such scientists as Glen Ruplinger has established that one's motor coordination, memory, attention, and mental performance are impaired by marijuana. This is evidenced by verbal confusion and the inability to communicate intelligently.

6. When high, a person's awareness of his self-identity and even of his body may lessen or completely vanish.

7. Marijuana causes one to lose self-control. It breaks down a person's moral inhibitions. It opens up one to commit sins which he would not normally commit.

8. While marijuana is not physically addictive, it can be psychologically addictive. Frequent users can become totally dependent upon marijuana for everyday living. Their first and last activity of the day is to smoke grass. These persons are called "potheads."

9. It is the pothead who faces the real danger of getting addicted to harder drugs. Marijuana creates a frame of mind or attitude which is conducive to further experimentation with stronger drugs. The user begins to desire stronger and longer drug experiences. Up to 95 percent of heroin users began with marijuana. It has been estimated that one out of five regular users of marijuana goes on to hard drugs. These users come into contact with harder drugs through pushers or at pot parties.

10. Marijuana opens up a person to demon possession. That it is possible to be taken over and controlled by Satan and his evil spirits is a part of the biblical world view.

One-fourth of the marijuana users who answered a questionnaire sent out by Charles Tate and reported in *Psychology Today* stated that during their marijuana-induced experience they were taken over and controlled by an evil person or power. About one-fourth of the users stated that they had become hostile, wicked, and antisocial. Over one-half of those questioned answered that they had experienced religious or spiritual sensations during which they met god or spiritual beings. These experiences are satanic in origin and pose the possible threat of demon possession.

In conclusion, marijuana can be psychologically addicting and harmful. It can impair the mental functions and generally produces an amotivational syndrome.

The physical effects of marijuana are not fully known at the present. But there is enough information to destroy the myth that marijuana is not physically harmful. This myth is incorrect on several accounts.

It is true that there is, at present, little evidence that marijuana will physically harm *infrequent users*; i.e., those who use it rarely—not every day or habitually. The only known injuries to infrequent users are inflamed, red eyes and irritated throat and lung tissue.

However, the counterculture is generally composed of frequent or heavy users of marijuana. And there is some evidence of physical harm to long-term users. This evidence is drawn from laboratory experiments and clinical observation of long-term users in drug-orientated communities such as Greenwich Village or in countries where the long-term use of marijuana has been carried on for generations.

According to several independent studies, the long-term use of marijuana can produce liver damage and bronchitis. There is some evidence that it may cause cancer. In laboratory animals, the long-term exposure of pregnant animals to marijuana has resulted in birth defects among the offspring. The mere possibility of malformed babies should prohibit the use of marijuana until further research has been performed. There may even be possible chromosomal damage from marijuana.

While these studies have not had sufficient time to establish the harmful effects of marijuana to everyone's satisfaction, they have discovered some serious dangers. We must remember that marijuana research is still in its infant stage; all the evidence is not in yet.

The social and economical effects of the use of marijuana are widely known. The infrequent user is not generally affected. He maintains his job and retains his sanity during the week. But the heavy user lives in a daze. He cannot be a productive member of society. He becomes dependent upon family, friends, panhandling, prostitution, or crime for money. He is a destructive force and an economic burden to society. His condition can be properly equated to the drunkards on skid row.

At the present, it is illegal in nearly thirty countries to possess or sell marijuana. This should discourage anyone from using this drug. God has instituted the state and instructed all men to be obedient to their governments in such matters (Romans 13:1-5; Titus 3:1; 1 Peter 2:13-15). That one fact alone should keep all who profess Christianity from using marijuana.

"But," someone may ask, "what if marijuana is legalized? Will this mean that we may use it?" The Christian must still say no. Even if it should be demonstrated that marijuana does not harm a person physically, it still produces a harmful mental state. The central issue of marijuana (and any other drug) is the drug experience itself. It is a sin against God, the world, society, and the individual person.

In conclusion, the use of marijuana is condemned by the Word of God. Those who rebel against God shall pay the eternal consequences.

A Marijuana Bibliography

A Federal Source Book: Answers to the Most Frequently Asked Questions About Drug Abuse. Chevy Chase, Maryland: National Clearinghouse for Drug Abuse Information, 1970, pp.7-12.

Adams, J.E. *The Big Umbrella.* Nutley, New Jersey: Presbyterian and Reformed Publishing Company, 1972, pp. 223-236.

Faltermayer, E.K. "What We Know About Marijuana—So Far." *Fortune.* no. 3, March 1971, pp. 92-98, 128-132.

Kolansky and Moore. "Toxic Effects of Chronic Marijuana Use." *Journal of American Medical Association*, 2, October 1972.

Lehmann, W.X. "Doctor, What About Marijuana?" *Reader's Digest.* April 1971, pp. 169-176.

Schaeffer, F.A. *The God Who Is There.* Chicago, Illinois: InterVarsity Press, 1968, pp. 27-29.

Smith, Wilder. *The Drug Users.* Wheaton, Illinois: Harold Shaw Publishers, 1969, pp. 59-78, 221, 254.

Solomon, D. *The Marijuana Papers.* Illinois: Bobs-Merrill, 1966.

Snyder, S. "Work With Marijuana: I. Effects." *Psychology Today.* no. 12, May 1971.

Tate, C. "Work With Marijuana: II. Sensations." *Psychology Today.* no. 12, May 1971.

Weil, A. "The Natural Mind—A New Way of Looking At the Higher Consciousness." *Psychology Today.* no. 5, October 1972.

DRUG CLASSIFICATION

Hallucinogens refer to such habituating psychedelic drugs as LSD, DMT, MDA, STP, mescaline, psilocybin, hashish, marijuana, belladonna, and morning glory seeds. They alter the mind's perception of the world, time, and one's self, and can result either in a state of euphoria or in a state of panic called a "bummer" or bad trip.

Stimulants usually refer to *amphetamines*, and include such drugs as speed, dexies, cocaine, bennies, pep-pills, ups, and so-called "diet" pills. These drugs reduce hunger and create a sensation of happiness or euphoria. They quicken the metabolism and can prevent sleep. They are addictive.

Sedatives are drugs which produce drowsiness and sleep. Such addictive drugs as Doriden, chloral hydrate, downers, sleepers, and goofballs are used to relieve tension. They are also sometimes used to come down from a high induced by a stimulant.

Tranquilizers are sometimes classed with sedatives. Such drugs as meprobamate, valium, placidyl, and librium calm and relax a person. They relieve and reduce anxiety and tension and may cause drowsiness. Some tranquilizers are addictive.

Barbiturates are like sedatives. They reduce anxiety and can cause sleep. An overdose will kill. They are addictive. Some of the popular barbiturates are barbital, membital, phenobarbital, and seconal.

Narcotics or *Opiates* are addictive drugs such as opium, heroin, morphine, methadone, meperidine, paregoric, codeine, and certain drugs found in strong cough syrups. These drugs have an analgesic property; i.e., they relieve pain. They also can cause sleep and generally depression. Some narcotics can cause sexual orgasm. They are addictive and an overdose will kill.

NOTES

Introduction

1. Wilder Smith, *The Drug Users* (Wheaton, IL: Harold Shaw Publishers, 1969), pp. 261-278.

Chapter 1

1. Andrew Weil, "The Natural Mind: A New Way of Looking at Drugs and the Higher Consciousness," *Psychology Today*, 6, no. 5 (October 1972), p. 66

2. Ibid., pp. 51-66, 83-96.

3. Richard de Lone, "The Ups and Downs of Drug Abuse Education," *Psychology Today*, 55, no. 46 (December 1972).

4. Weil, "The Natural Mind," pp. 51-66, 83-96.

5. Timothy Leary, "The Principles and Practice of Hedonic Psychology," *Psychology Today*, 6, no. 3 (January 1973).

Chapter 2

1. F.A. Schaeffer, *Pollution and the Death of Man* (Wheaton, IL: Tyndale House, 1970).

2. Lit-sen Chang, *Zen-Existentialism* (Nutley, NJ: Presbyterian and Reformed Publishing Co., 1969), pp. 1-25, 210-227.

3. Schaeffer, *Genesis in Space and Time* (Downers

Grove, IL: InterVarsity Press, 1972), pp. 13-66; P.E. Hughes, *Christianity and the Problem of Origins* (Nutley, NJ: Presbyterian and Reformed Publishing Co., 1964); R.J. Rushdoony, *The Biblical Philosophy of History* (Nutley, NJ: Presbyterian and Reformed Publishing Co., 1969); E.J. Young, *Studies in Genesis One* (Nutley, NJ: Presbyterian and Reformed Publishing Co., 1964).

Chapter 3

1. F.A. Schaeffer, *Genesis in Space and Time* (Downers Grove, IL: InterVarsity Press, 1972), pp. 69-101; Gardner, Cheeseman, Sadgrove and Wright, *The Grace of God in the Gospel* (London: The Banner of Truth Trust, 1972), pp. 33-41; J.B. Machen, *The Christian View of Man* (London: The Banner of Truth Trust, 1969), pp. 161-232.

Chapter 4

1. Gardner, Cheeseman, Sadgrove and Wright, *The Grace of God in the Gospel* (London: The Banner of Truth Trust, 1972), pp. 33-41; J.G. Machen, *The Christian View of Man* (London: The Banner of Truth Trust, 1969); J. Murray, *Redemption Accomplished and Applied* (Grand Rapids: Wm. B. Eerdmans Publishing Co., 1968); F.A. Schaeffer, *Genesis in Space and Time* (Downers Grove, IL: InterVarsity Press, 1972), pp. 103-160; J.H. Thornwell, *Election and Reprobation* (Nutley, NJ: Presbyterian and Reformed Publishing Co., 1961).

2. Lit-sen Chang, *Zen-Existentialism* (Nutley, NJ: Presbyterian and Reformed Publishing Co., 1969), pp. 1-25, 79-113, 151-172, 210-217.

Chapter 5

1. G.H. Clark, *A Christian View of Men and Things* (Grand Rapids, MI: Wm. B. Eerdmans Publishing Co., 1951), pp. 151-196; J. Murray, *Principles of Conduct* (Grand Rapids, MI: Wm. B. Eerdmans Publishing Co., 1957); C. Van Til, *Christian Theistic Evidences* (Philadelphia, PA: Westminster Theological Seminary, 1964).

2. F.A. Schaeffer, *The God Who Is There* (Chicago, IL: InterVarsity Press, 1968), pp. 27-29; S. Snyder, "The True Speed Trip: Schizophrenia," *Psychology Today*, 5, no. 8 (January 1972).

Chapter 6

1. M.F. Unger, *Demons in the World Today* (Wheaton, IL: Tyndale House Publishers, 1971), pp. 10-13, 75-76; *The Zondervan Pictorial Dictionary* (Grand Rapids, MI: Zondervan Publishing House, 1963), pp. 501-502.

2. See A. Deissman, *Light From the Ancient East* (New York, NY: George A. Doran Co., 1909), p. 259 for an example of a drug formula in a magic book.

3. Kitto, ed., *A Cyclopedia of Biblical Literature* (New York, NY: William H. Moore and Co., 1846) p. 959.

4. *Baker's Dictionary of Theology* (Grand Rapids, MI: Baker Book House, 1960), p.555.

5. A.T. Robertson, *Word Pictures in the New Testament* (Nashville, TN: Broadman Press, 1931), 4:313.

6. W. Braden, *The Private Sea: LSD and the Search for God* (Chicago, IL: Quadrangle Books, 1967), pp. 54-55.

7. Unger, *Demons.* (Tyndale House Publishers, 1971).

8. *A Federal Source Book: Answers to the Most Frequently Asked Questions About Drug Abuse* (Chevy Chase, MD: National Clearinghouse for Drug Abuse Information, 1970), p. 2; *Drugs: Insights and Illusion* (USA: Scholastic Book Services), p. 15.

9. Such scholars as Alford, Kitto, Lange, Lenski, A.T. Robertson, Vincent, etc.

10. James Orr, ed., *International Standard Bible Encyclopedia* (Grand Rapids, MI: Wm. B. Eerdmans Publishing Co., 1939), 5:3097.

11. R.C.H. Lenski, *The Interpretation of St. Paul's Epistles to the Galatians, Ephesians, and Philippians* (Minneapolis, MN: Augsburg Publishing House, 1961), p. 286; Robertson, *Word Pictures* 4:313; Martin R. Vincent, *Word Studies in the New Testament* (Grand Rapids, MI: Wm. B. Eerdmans Publishing Co., 1969), 4:165.

12. Roger Nicole, ed., *The Expositor's Greek New Testament* (Grand Rapids, MI: Wm. B. Eerdmans Publishing Co., 1967), 4:187.

13. J.B. Lange, *Lange's Commentary on the Holy Scriptures* (Grand Rapids, MI: Zondervan Publishing House, 1960), 11:138.

14. J.B. Lightfoot, *The Epistle of Paul to the Galatians* (Grand Rapids, MI: Zondervan Publishing House, 1962), p. 210.

15. H. Alford, *The Greek New Testament* (Chicago, IL: Moody Press, 1968), 4:648; see also: Robertson, *Word Pictures,* 6:369.

16. Unger, *Demons;* J.L. Nevius, *Demon Possession* (Grand Rapids, MI: Kregel Publications, 1968).

17. A. Watts, *The Joyous Cosmology* (New York, NY: Vintage Books, 1962), p. 93.

18. Robertson, *Word Pictures,* 6:445; Lenski, *The Interpretation of St. John's Revelation* (Minneapolis, MN: Augsburg Publishing House, 1963), p. 533.

19. A.E. Wilder Smith, *The Drug User* (Wheaton, IL: Harold Shaw Publishers, 1969), pp. 261-278; Timothy Leary, *The Politics of Ecstasy* (New York, NY: Putnam Publishing Company, 1968).

20. Lange, *Lange's Commentary,* p. 138.

Chapter 7

1. A. Watts, *The Joyous Cosmology* (New York, NY: Vintage Books, 1962), pp. xi,xviii, 18, 19, 90.

2. F.A. Schaeffer, *The God Who Is There* (Downers Grove, IL: InterVarsity Press, 1968), pp. 27-29.

3. F.A. Schaeffer, *Escape from Reason* (Downers Grove, IL: InterVarsity Press, 1968), pp. 46-55

4. W. Braden, *The Private Sea: LSD and the Search for God* (Chicago, IL: Quadrangle Books, 1967), pp. 117-119.

5. F.A. Schaeffer, *The God Who Is There; Escape from Reason;* and *He Is There and He Is Not Silent* (Wheaton, IL: Tyndale House Publishers, 1972).

6. J.G. Machen, *What Is Faith* (Grand Rapids, MI: Wm. B. Eerdmans Publishing Co., 1965).

Chapter 8

1. F.A. Schaeffer, *Pollution and the Death of Man* (Wheaton, IL: Tyndale House Publishers, 1970), pp. 47-64.

2. W. Braden, *The Private Sea: LSD and the Search for God* (Chicago, IL: Quadrangle Books, 1967), pp. 22-25.

3. *A Federal Source Book: Answers to the Most Frequently Asked Questions About Drug Abuse* (Chevy Chase, MD: National Clearinghouse for Drug Abuse Information), see Appendix A.

Chapter 9

1. F.A. Schaeffer, *Genesis in Space and Time* (Downers Grove, IL: InterVarsity Press, 1972), pp. 13-52.

2. Andrew Weil, "The Natural Mind: A New Way of Looking at Drugs and the Higher Consciousness, "*Psychology Today*, 6, no.5 (October 1972), 83.

3. A. Watts, *The Joyous Cosmology* (New York, NY: Vintage Books, 1962).

4. A.E. Wilder Smith, *The Drug Users* (Wheaton, IL: Harold Shaw Publishers, 1969), pp. 233-260.

Chapter 10

1. Lit-sen Chang, *Zen-Existentialism* (Nutley, NJ: Presbyterian and Reformed Publishing Co., 1969), p. 14.

2. "LSD and Broken Chromosomes," *The Sciences*, 8, no. 1 (January 1968); Jacobson and Berlin, "LSD and Human Reproduction," *Journal of American Medical Association* (December 1972); A.E. Wilder Smith, *The Drug Users* (Wheaton, IL: Harold Shaw Publishers, 1969), pp. 26-27.

3. M. Rogers, "Drug Abuse by Prescription," *Psychology Today*, 5, no. 11 (September 1971).

Chapter 11

1. S. Arterburn and J. Burns, *Drug-Proof Your Kids* (Pomona, CA: Focus on the Family, 1989), p. 108.

2. The Banner of Truth Trust, London.

3. The Presbyterian and Reformed Publishing Co., Nutley, NJ 1971.

4. The Presbyterian and Reformed Publishing Co., Nutley, NJ.

Chapter 12

1. The Banner of Truth Trust, London.

Other Good
Harvest House Reading

FATAL ATTRACTIONS
by *Bill Perkins*

From the beginning of history men and women have struggled with "fatal attractions," secret thoughts and behaviors that pull them away from God and each other. In *Fatal Attractions* author Bill Perkins shows how readers can break free from these hidden addictions by allowing God to fill the empty places that obsessive behaviors occupy. He leads the reader to an understanding of the hopelessness of quick-fix solutions and offers a workable, biblical plan of action for overcoming the power of unhealthy desires.

THE TRUTH ABOUT MASONS
by *Robert A. Morey*

Is the Masonic Lodge a Christian fraternity or an occult organization? Can you be a Christian *and* a Mason? These questions are generating conflict throughout the evangelical church and fueling a growing civil war within Masonry itself. Noted researcher Robert Morey presents historical documentation that gets to the heart of these critical issues.

ISLAMIC INVASION
by *Robert Morey*

Islam—once an obscure Middle Eastern religion—has rapidly grown into the second largest religion in the world. Robert Morey, one of Christianity's clearest communicators on Muslim belief, gives you the insight you need to understand Islam and the challenge it poses today.